Instagram Impactor:

Marketing & Branding to Attract the Right Followers to Your Business!

By: Marlinda Davis

Instagram Impactor: Marketing & Branding to Attract the Right Followers to Your Business!

Copyright © 2016 by Marlinda Davis.

All rights reserved. No part of this book may be reproduced in any form without permission in writing from the author. Reviewers may quote brief passages in reviews.

Copyright & Disclaimer

Copyright ©2016 by Marlinda Davis. All rights reserved.

Published by Marlinda Davis. Salisbury, North Carolina.

No part in this publication may be reproduced, stored in a retrieval system or transmitted in any form or by any means, mechanical, photocopying, recording, scanning, electronic, or otherwise, except as permitted under section 107 or 108 of the 1976 United States Copyright Act without the prior permission of the publisher.

Limit of Liability/Disclaimer of Warranty: While the publisher and author have made all attempts to verify the information provided in this publication, neither the author nor the publisher assumes any responsibility for errors, omissions, or contrary interpretations of the subject matter herein. This book is for entertainment purposes only. The views expressed are those of the author alone, and should not be taken as expert instruction or commands. The reader is responsible for his/her own actions. Adherence to all applicable laws and regulations, including international, federal, state and local governing professional licensing, business practices, advertising, and all other aspects of doing business in the U.S., Canada or any other jurisdiction is the sole responsibility of the purchaser or reader.

Trademarked names appearing in this book may not always be followed by a trademark symbol. The names are used in an editorial fashion and to the benefit of the trademark owner, with no intention of infringement of the trademark. The information in this book is distributed on an "as is" basis, without warranty of any kind, either expressed or implied.

The advice and strategies contained herein may not be suitable for your situation. Neither the publisher nor the author shall be liable for any loss of profit or other commercial damages, including, but not limited to, special, incidental, consequential or other damages.

Table of Contents

Preface

Chapter 1: Insta-basics

Chapter 2: Insta-posting

Chapter 3: Insta-followers

Chapter 4: Insta-connections

Conclusion

Bibliography

Preface

I first heard about Instagram through a google search I think. It's been a while, but I was looking for ways to grow my business. At that time, I was affiliated with a network marketing company. It was in 2013, and since the company was beauty related, it is almost obvious how pictures were definitely the best media available. I could undoubtedly use them in order to illustrate products and results whether it be the packaging, a look book, or some other form of display. Without hesitation, I immediately signed up since it was, and still is, a free platform since the potential was there looking at me square in the eyes. Once I had the account, I thought if I just posted some gorgeous pictures that the customers would come rolling in. How could they resist, right?

Wrong! The problem with my plan was that I had no idea on how to actually use this platform. I became increasingly frustrated because no one was seeing my posts. My business was failing but the dormant potential of this medium burned away at my soul like a furnace blazing in the middle of winter. So I did what any good, determined business person would do. I began to research. I bought books, looked at videos, read websites and interviewed some people to figure out all of the ins and outs of using this, deceptively, straight forward app. I learned all about gaining followers, following other Instagrammers, tags, tracking my activity, consistency, and so much more that I had no idea about when I first started. I learned the importance of including a call to action and other strategies to gain followers. Ok, I have to callout the elephant in the room, stay far faaaaarrrrrr away from get followers fast schemes aka bots but I'll talk about them in further details later.

As my knowledge grew, so did my business and I was able to share so much more than that with my online network who became more like my family! Instagram completely changed my life and my business and I want to also share my gift of knowledge with as much people as I can. I have since moved on from that business to becoming a full-time Instagram consultant but it is my wish that everyone has every opportunity at success which is my inspiration for writing this and a series of books that will focus on Instagram and other social media platforms. Many people do not realize the true power of sharing their story through social media.

Your story is what sets you apart from everyone else. That includes your business but also your life, family, travel, faith, hobbies and other things that make up your persona. People connect with someone they can relate to which builds trust which makes them more likely to do business with *you* instead of one of your competitors. The market and world as a whole is changing so we must change along with it or be left behind.

I had to dig up the information the hard way but it is my hope that I can ease some of that burden from you. I make no claims to guarantee your success but I do hope that you use this information, along with hard work in your respective field to catapult you in the right direction in reaching your goals. You need to use this information to attract the right people among other things. As I mentioned before, this is the first of, hopefully, a series of books on Instagram and social media.

I know I am not perfect and for this reason, I value your feedback. If you enjoyed this book let me know by the way of leaving a review. If there was something you think I can improve on, let me know also. Also share this book with anyone who is working on building their Instagram account! Thank you so much for entrusting me to guide you in the right direction and it is my genuine goal to do as much as I can. God bless and best wishes on your endeavors ☺

Chapter 1: Insta-basics

Currently, there are upwards of 150 million *active* users, worldwide on Instagram. According to eMarketer.com, in 2014, for the US alone saw 64.2 million users on Instagram. It is projected that by 2019, this number will have almost doubled! If ever there was a time to get your business(es) on Instagram, *right now* is it!

Before you even think about creating your account, there are a few steps you need to take. This is because you want to make sure that the information you are putting out is representative of your brand and what your message is. Are you targeting a specific niche like moms over 30 struggling with weight loss or are you trying to spread awareness to the overall population about cancer or sustainable development? Here are a few questions you need to answer before creating your account.

1) Why did you decide to use Instagram as a promotional tool?
2) Who are you trying to reach out to?
3) What is your purpose? (ie. Selling, informing, buying, petitioning, etc.)
4) How will your brand be visually represented? (ie. Color scheme, filters, specific fonts, etc.)
5) What brands does your brand connect with? (ie. If you were having a business party, which brands would you invite?)

Write down the answers to each of these questions and be as detailed as you want to be. The more detailed the better because they will set the foundation to build your brand and identity on. It will also help you when reaching out to new clients because you will be organized and structured which will leave a positive impression on your prospect. Lastly, it will help you formulate a list of other brands you might want to network with and model.

Do not copy any brand verbatim but you will find that the brands that people follow tend to have the same vibe to them so don't be afraid to pick up on key components from a brand that you think your potential client might like also. At the same time, you still want to stand out from those other brands. Your goal is to make your brand fit in with the clique but to be identifiable *without* its name attached.

A great example of this is Coca-cola. Their colors are red and white while their message is to get out and have fun. Their brands are always full of laughter, adventure, and sharing what they are passionate about. So their Instagram pictures always reflect that. The brands they align with reflect that also so how does Coca-cola stand out? With their iconic colors but also with their iconic coke bottle(s) that they make sure show in nearly every shot whether it be a photo or video even if it is in the background. It will take some time and a few tries but you will also find ways to make your brand stand out from your competitors as well.

Instagram is accessible on any device, however, it is limited to viewing user feeds and commenting on photos when used outside of your mobile phone. In order to have full access, you will need to use it on your mobile phone. The Instagram phone app can be downloaded from [iTunes](#) if you are on an apple device or from [Google Play Store](#) if you are on an android device. Click the above links to take you to download the app for your respective device. Follow the prompts and Instagram should be installed after a couple of clicks.

The name of your account is very important. While you have the freedom to be as creative as you want, you should keep in mind your business and branding when deciding on your account's name. If it is for your business, use its name for your account. If your username is a popular choice then try adding underscores or dashes to make a unique version or add your initials to the beginning or end. For example, suppose you are a fitness instructor and your business name is Fitness For All. This is pretty generic so the username fitnessforall is likely taken already. Some options might be fitness_for_all, fitness_4_all, fitnessforall_mcd, and so on. Your username *is* part of your branding so make sure that it coincides. Don't assume your username is taken right away. During the sign-in process you will find out if it is available. Have a few variations just in case but hopefully you get the one you want!

Once you have your account setup and branding in place, make sure that you actually post. If you do not have the time to post, there are a number of outsourcing methods that you can take advantage of. I also give you some services that will help in subsequent chapters. Be sure that you are consistent and engaging with your audience. Just like any other social media, if you are not active, you will lose followers and your account might be shutdown. Also, think about this, if you have an account that you are not using, you could be potentially hindering someone else's business by having the username they wanted. So make it worth your while or wait until you are ready to make the commitment!

Chapter 2: Insta-Posting

Make sure posts are in focus and easy to see. Good lighting.

Now that you have everything setup, you are probably starting to think about posting. What should you post? When is the best time to post? Should you be more or less personal with your posts? Should you focus more on your brand or yourself? The answer to these questions depends on the nature of your business as well as the message that you want to convey through your Instagram account. I can tell you that it takes some time and experimentation to find what works for you and what your audience or clients enjoy. Don't be afraid to try new things or posts that you like on other people/company pages. Different people have different opinions but here are my thoughts on these matters.

In general, there are two kinds of business. One where you personally provide service and one where your business provides the service. In my experience, it is important to focus on branding, however, *you* are what sets your business apart from others so don't be afraid to post something personal once in a while. Of course, depending on your branding you don't want to overdo it but if all else fails, ask in a call-to-action for your audience to tell you what they like the most. You might have to ask them in different ways like what motivates them if you are a health and fitness professional, what inspires them if you are in the arts or be straightforward and ask if they would tell you in the comments section what they think of your content.

When and What to Post.

The answers to these questions are dependent on your audience and the nature of your business. Experiment with posting times and take note of when you get the most post engagement. There are a bunch of apps and services that will analyze your Instagram statistics like audience engagement but personally my rule of thumb is three time per day. On in the morning (9am), one in the afternoon (12pm) and one in the evening (7-9pm). Most analytics services do not specialize in Instagram but they are still none the less essential to getting to know your audience and how you can best serve them. Some of my favorites are:

- SimplyMeasured – I like this service because they offer free and paid resources. This means that you can at least get a start in planning your marketing strategies not just on Instagram but other social media platforms as well.

- IconoSquare (formerly Statigram) – This service is Instagram only and only offers a 7 day free-trial. Like most Instagram only services, it is sort of pricey in comparison to some others but you can get detailed reports which will help you track viewer engagement and other information that is important to consider when posting. To me, it is worth the money because you will be able to fully optimize your Instagram marketing.

- [Crowdfire (formerly JustUnfollow)](#) – I recommend this one as a beginner. It is free, works on all devices and produces excellent reports.

Now once you have figured out when the best time is to post, make sure you post! And make sure you post EVERY day! SO many people think they can take a day off but that doesn't apply when you are trying to run a business. Just like you need to be working your business every day, you need to be posting every day also. Remember, not everyone is on at the same time so different people may see your post each time. Consistency will get you clients and set you apart from your competition. Never underestimate the power of consistency.

If you are struggling with finding time to post when you need to there are now scheduling services available for Instagram, however, they are not free. Some offer a free trial period but it is worth it in my opinion. Don't get hung up on having to pay though because it will pay for itself in the long run. If you're not willing to invest in your business you're not going to get far. Here are a couple of my recommendations:

- <u>Later (formerly Latergrammed)</u> – Later is almost like an organizational tool since you still have to manually post your media but it allows you to visually see what your week or month of posts will look like. It will notify you to post whenever you schedule it like an alarm clock.

- <u>Schedugram</u> – Schedugram is really simple to use. You can schedule both images and video, have multiple accounts linked to one Schedugram account, multiple users can access the account, and you can have notifications sent to your e-mail inbox once they post.

Same or Separate Accounts?

I get asked this question all the time but the answer is always different for each individual situation. For example, say you run a photography business where YOU are the photographer taking pictures. This is considered a business where you personally provide the service. In this case, you have the freedom to post personal and business posts because you want your clients and potential clients to get to know you. You are the brand of this type of business. Some other examples of personal businesses are coaching, illustrating, writing under your name, and baby/pet sitting.

An additional benefit to having an account setup this way is that it works as your personal resume or/and portfolio. It is easily accessed on any device that can connect to the internet whether it is mobile or not. Remember, Instagram feeds can be accessed on the computer so if you are a freelance photographer, artist, baker, chef, or even writer, don't forget to add your Instagram url to your business card as well. Clients will get to see your best self and your best work. It does not take long before a person figures out whether they do or do not like (or trust) you so you want to be sure to make a strong case right away. At the same time, you probably aren't going to want to post that drunk picture of you from a party last Friday night or one your spouse took first thing in the morning before you combed your hair. If you want to posts pictures like that, then I would suggest making a separate account in all cases. Keep it professional but show your human side also.

Another example is if you are selling photographic equipment you might want to post less about yourself and more about the products, photography, and company branding. I would still include personal posts but definitely more photography tailored. For instance, take a picture of you taking a picture with a DSLR camera you have in stock then explain why it is superior or equivalent to other cameras. Demonstrate your knowledge without making yourself the focus because you're selling products not you. Post around the company branding while still adding your personal touch.

Of course, if you are concerned about a potential conflict of interest just make two separate accounts. There is a function where you can add multiple accounts so that you can easily switch between them on the same device without having to log in and out just like google accounts. If you choose to do that just add your personal account in the comments section. In my experience, you don't want to hide behind the company because people relate to people not a company.

You will likely make several changes before you find what works. The good thing is that it is easy and free to make an account so even if you made two separate accounts the found out that your brand works better as one solid account there's no harm done. Or you might find out that you want to break up your company into different sectioned accounts that point to one master account. The sky is the limit! Make the most out of it.

Hashtags

Hashtags are part of the Instagram culture that is widely abused. The point of a hashtag is to 'tag' your post in a stream of posts under that word so that people who search that word see the posts in order of most recently posted. In order to hashtag a post, you simply put a pound symbol before the word with no spaces between the pound and each word. For instance, if you are a fitness instructor and your post is demonstrating squats. You may hashtag booty goals (#bootygoals) and another one fitlife (#fitlife).

For each hashtag page, the top 9 posts are pinned to the top of the feed. Then underneath them are the most recent posts as of when you searched the hashtag. If the hashtag is very popular like #fitlife, the feed will be continuously changing by the second which means that if you were to refresh the page, it may look completely different than what you first saw. On the other hand, if the hashtag is less used like #bootygoals, the feed might not change as fast.

A rule of thumb for tags is to use no more than 5-10 per post. After that it can look unprofessional and spamy. Make sure to separate your hashtags from the main post. You can do this with periods or dashes stacked on top of each other or in an ellipses style. For example:

- …

    start hashtags here

- -

    -

    -

    start hashtags here

There is not a specific rule so choose whichever style works for you and your brand. You can even ask your followers if *they* prefer one style over the other. Even though this might seem like a small detail, it can earn you big time brownie points with your viewer because it shows that you care about what they think.

You can also create your own hashtags as part of your brand for followers who want to see your stuff and most importantly posts of other clients using your product or showing their results of your service. This will allow you to gain credibility and trust from skeptical followers who are interested in your business. A great example of this would be to hold a contest where the prize is a product, coupon, or some sort of gift in exchange for them posting using your specific hashtag on a picture of them using a product or their results.

Another great use for hashtags is to promote a new product. You can use a certain hashtag to act as a teaser which will help you gain traction, interest and excitement around its release. Be sure to mention that your users should check out the hashtag to see more somewhere on your post. Remember, all your previous posts that are tagged with the same hashtag will always be there so you don't necessarily have to repost old posts unless it was a really big hit.

Geotagging

Geotagging is similar to hashtags but instead of a word or phrase, it is a location. So for instance, if you are a fitness gym in Charlotte, NC. You can geotag your location or a location near you to attract followers in the area to your gym. This is a very powerful tool when used correctly.

Connecting to Other Social Media

There are a number of social media platforms that you can connect to your Instagram account like Facebook, Flickr, and Twitter. This is great because it can save you time on posting, however, I don't recommend making it a habit. Reason being, if your followers follow you on other social media, there is not any need or value for them to follow you on your Instagram account. Also, different media work best on different social media platforms. For example, Facebook is good for long videos while Instagram only supports short clips. Your viewers on Facebook might be looking for more information than can be presented in a 30 minute short.

Chapter 3: Insta-Followers

So now that you're all set with posting its time to get some people to see your post and network with! No, they don't just show up on your page and not all the time they follow you right away. Don't fall into the buying follower scams either. Those are not real followers and often times get banned in large numbers so it's a huge waste of money which at the end of the day is not bringing you customers. Remember, the goal of your Instagram account is to bring you new or potential clients who are interested in what you have to offer.

In order to get followers, you are going to have to do a bit of planning. The first thing you need to consider is timing. I touched on this before but posting consistently with time will train your followers to look for your posts at a specific time *every* day. Additionally, it keeps your followers engaged in your network so that they do not easily forget about you and move on to a competitor's site. You are also proving *your* worth by proving to your followers that you are organized, consistent and dedicated to providing quality content, services, etc.

Once you have attracted your followers to the page, you need to be able to keep them. To do this you need to ensure that you are producing entertaining content. Do not post the same pictures over and over again, especially in a close time frame. If you are having a bit of a creative block, do a quick search online for your niche and end it with IG post to see what shows up. You might also look at competitor or fan pages that you enjoy in your niche and glean ideas from them. Do not settle for I don't know what to post or you will fall off of your game and that will not be good for your business. Now if you have a post that was 6 months ago, you can use that again but still find a way to make it new and engaging.

The key to Instagram is images so in order to attract new followers you need to have great pictures. This does not mean that you need to go out and buy the most expensive photography equipment and lighting. You can use your phone camera but make sure that the lights are turned on. Also, make sure that the focus of the picture is in focus. For instance, if you are a gym owner and you are taking a picture of one of your trainers working with a client and there are various weights way in the background. Make sure that your camera is focused on the trainer and client instead of the weights way in the background. Additionally, you want to make sure that the picture has color contrast. By this, I mean to make sure that colors stand out from each other. For instance, make sure that the outfits the trainer and client are wearing are not the same color as the walls that surround them. This not only makes the picture more interesting but it makes it appealing to someone who is color blind or impaired.

Another way to attract new followers is through using creative hashtags. If you do not know what they are, be sure to go back and read the section where I talk about them. By using a mix of popular and created hashtags, you will be able to attract more followers especially when they start using your hashtags and all of their followers see it as well. Just make sure that it is related to your brand and post.

If you are not getting in followers like you want to using these methods then you are going to have to purposely search and find people that you think would be interested in you and your product, service or whatever it is you are selling. This is a skill that will take some time to develop and you might even feel awkward doing it at first but…let's face it…we all do it anyways right? Yes, on Facebook when you see one of your friends tagged by another person who isn't your friend but you know and want to see what they've been up to so you click their name and stalk through their page to find out that they got married and live in New Mexico with five children before 25! Sounds like a happy couple to me *wink, wink* OK, lol, sorry my perversion monster showed its ugly head for a minute but you get the point right? Don't overcomplicate the process. Just do it!

This next one might seem common sense since this *is* social networking but be sure to always respond to *all* comments. Do not pick favorites or comment to some and not others. This will only create a rift between you and your followers that may cause them to turn off of your page and go to another. By answering to comments you not only engage with your followers, you show potential followers that you are present in your social account and it's not just run by some bot somewhere.

Another common sense activity that you need to be doing is socializing with other pages on Instagram. Make sure that you are liking posts and leaving nice comments. Even tag some friends you think might enjoy the media. People who visit that person's page will also see your name and click on to your account. There are services like Instagress that you can use to post comments but I caution against that because there are always instances when the comment does not fit the picture. The user of the picture can flag you as a spammer and your account can potentially be banned as a result.

Chapter 4: Insta-Connections

One thing that is so great about social networking is that you can point your followers to where you want them to be so that they can see what you want them to see. It's almost like taking a huge chunk out of the wait and frustration of catching a fish. Of course, you're not always going to catch the fish but you will catch a lot more than sitting and waiting for it to happen upon your bait.

If you have a blog or website, you can embed a video from your Instagram onto your site. By doing this, people who view the video and like your feed will follow your Instagram account to see more of what you have to offer. By seeing more of your brand they might like it and be more likely to purchase something than if they only viewed one video on your website or blog.

Another way to connect with potential and current followers is to make sure to include a call-to-action. This will prompt them to do something. Whether it is to let you know what they want to see more of, what they like to do on the weekend, or what they think of some new product you just launched, ask them a question that they will have to provide a written response to. Then you can carry on a conversation in the comments. Again, this will show your followers that you are a real person and not just an emotionless, robot. Trust is one of your biggest allies in social networking so if you can find a way to build it, do it!

Some basic housekeeping is essential to providing a clean, clear first impression. Always make sure that your bio and profile are filled out completely. It only takes a couple of seconds before a user determines whether they like you or not. You do not want to give them reason to click off your page without even getting to the good stuff. Also, remember that there are all sorts of scammers and predators out there so if you portray yourself as such, even though you are not, you will have the same reaction since that is what you are putting out there.

Don't be afraid to open up to your followers. No, don't run around in your underclothes but show them your human side. Show them the barbecue set up for July 4th or the birth of your second child or even grandchild. People want to feel included and accepted. It might take them a while but eventually they will turn into future customers because if they are following you it is because they are interested in you!

Conclusion

When I first started Instagram, I was clueless in both how to use it and its full potential in my business. I hope that I have given you a framework to actively use in your social media journey whether it be for business, personal or a bit of both. As I mentioned in the beginning of this book, I do plan on continuing to write instructional books on other social media platforms of which I hope you read as well. Social networking is truly networking in the most beautiful and creative sense.

As the author of this book, in addition to it being one of my first professional publications, I value your feedback. I am always looking to improve so that I can better help you and make my future publications even more awesome. That being said, let me know the things you really enjoyed while reading. Also, let me know if there was anything you did not like or any fixes that I need to make. Leave these comments as a review under the amount of stars you rate this publication. Thanks again for your time and diligence!

Now get out there and make a big impact with media on Instagram!

See you soon,

Marlinda Davis ☺

Bibliography

"Instagram Will Top 100 Million US Users by 2018". *eMarketer.com*.

Web. July 17, 2016.

www.ingramcontent.com/pod-product-compliance
Lightning Source LLC
Chambersburg PA
CBHW071828200526
45169CB00018B/1234